To Dance Down Winter

To Dance Down Winter

poems by

Martha Moore

Black Hat Press
Goodhue, Minnesota
1995

ACKNOWLEDGMENTS

Some of these poems previously appeared in *Wisconsin Academy Review, Wisconsin Academy Conference Proceedings, Wisconsin Review, Fox Cry, Heartland Journal, Wisconsin Poets' Calendar,* and in the anthologies *Looking Out the Window* and *A View From the Edge.*

Cover photo by Ron Harrell
from an oil painting by Merton Grenhagen

ISBN: 1-887649-03-4

Published by BLACK HAT PRESS
Post Office Box 12
Goodhue, Minnesota 55027
All rights reserved

Printed in the United States of America

CONTENTS

I

VOICES IN THE HOUSE

II

LIGHT IN THE DARKNESS

For Laurel Mills and Gladys Veidemanis, who helped me hone my words, and special thanks to Helen Fahrbach and Marilyn Potter.

alas, for each invisible drop of water which I drink sleepily
and for each sound which I receive, trembling,
I have the same absent thirst and the same cold fever . . .

—PABLO NERUDA, *Ars Poetica*

I

VOICES IN THE HOUSE

Patiently the Singer Waits

On a far fence,
a bluebird box lined
with thorns, leaves, grass.

All winter it bears
the sob of wind;
in early spring the throb of rain.

Then . . . three pale eggs,
safe from cat,
hawk, starling.

Patiently the singer waits
the crack of shell,
the breaking out of beaks

that open wide for lumpy
spider ball with spine
of walking stick inside,

for currant flesh
and seed of ash
or mulberry.

Voices in the House Where I Was Born

A strange, strange thing—
in this house where I was born
this morning's spring!

—Issa

My grandson Andy, who loves to start the hearts
of rusted cars and probe the secret selves
of gadgets, has discovered a small Victorian mouth-
      piece
which wafted voices through my childhood long before
the birth of intercoms. Fragile, jonquil shaped,
it has jutted all my life from the upstairs hall.

Andy peers into it as he would the engine
of a 1912 Stanley Steamer: "Look, Gramma, I'll bet
we could still use this old-time walky-talky.
I saw a hole next to the back door
that's probably its other end. I'll run down
and blow it free. You listen."

Even though I know that plaster dust
and chunks of wall have sealed this aged ear,
I press my own, deaf as stone, upon it.
But all I hear are memories. Six again,
too old to be told to nap, I've climbed a stool
to listen at the mouthpiece for a whisper

like oak leaves rasping the house in fall.
But voices of napless children snicker up
teasing me to sneak behind Miss Pickett's fence.
Which they know I'd never dare to. Instead, I'm
      waiting

to float to islands in the sky on a purple barge
no one else can see, that's lined with satin pillows
and feather boas like those in Arthur Rackham's book
beside my bed. I'm listening for the voice that cautions:
Hold your breath. It's almost time to jump.
The barge is circling Farley's roof now. Creep
to your window like a cat. If no grownup sees you,
not a soul will know about your floating, unless you tell.

I remember how I kept it secret—even from myself—
afraid of wagging heads. Now that Andy's
brought it back, I want to shout it
down the dear old crumbling intercom and bless
his heart for starting mine, but I'm sure no voice
could penetrate the plaster wall of time.

Suddenly a half-boy, half-man chuckle
caroms up like the chug of a Model T:
"Gramma, can ya hear me now?
I've blown it free."

Recurring Dream

Night after night, my own eyes peer
from the face of my father as he floats
on a raft of splintery elm under wild purple sky,
beseeches us in his thin child's voice,
    "Let me go.
      Let me go."

But we reel him in, smooth splinters,
splice his fraying anchor rope—
our backs to strong white arms
of the beckoning wave rising
to wrap him in silken skeins

and swirl his bones
down, down
to emerald grottos
where small boys not yet born
wait to be called in from play.

My Father's Dark

A chained terrier jangles his irritation
along a clothesline. Two jays scream
from gnarled and jagged oaks.

Beyond the backyard fence a captive plane,
lashed to a grinning boy, shrieks
as it gyrates in an endless arc.

Strapped to his wheelchair from crotch to chin,
my father—once patriarch
to every shrub of his sculpted lawn—

peers inward at the vacant lot
that is his mind, no longer dreams
of clipping wayward ramblers

rioting the southeast hedge,
of banking with floribunda snow
the cannas raising crimson swords
against the sun.

My Father's Light

for Charles Henry Williams, 1873–1959

It was my father I saw this morning
in the gold of the shagbark hickory.
How could there be such light
in all that dark?

Most of the year black-brown leaves,
like desiccated bat wings,
haunt the windows of my memory:
my father's eyes, his thin child's voice
begging me to let him go, let him go;
his bent fingers, one poked out
like a broken twig, clutching
a *Life* or *Time* upside down.

But today there he was, holding
a little map of where to trade—
a coreopsis for an aster,
a pansy for a lily—and telling me
I was old enough to be his partner
in "The Plant Exchange." No money in it:
only pride and a fellow feeling
for growing things.

I'd pull my wagonload of long-legged
canna roots to the corner of Vine and Cherry,
and return with leeks from Wales
Mrs. Owen Thomas swore
would top Scottish thistles any day.

Up Spruce and Cedar, over Congress
past the mill, down High Street,
then the boulevard and home.
All the way I'd be smiling
in my father's light.

Bird Bones

for Sarah Crocker Smith, 1814–1883

Great-grandmother, both you and your daughter—
my namesake grandma—died before I was born.
I know you only from my father's tales:

you cradled one-year-old Martha,
bumping from New York to Wisconsin
in a covered wagon drawn by two white horses.

At last, huddled in a cold log cabin,
you warmed your soul in books:
sought out tracts and disquisitions
on the good life, read romances
by Tennyson and Sir Walter Scott.
More and more you sought your answers

from vagrant winds.
When Martha married and moved to town
you must have flown with her

for you were there sending my father
for sugar lumps to Charlie Russell's store
when he was four, and teaching him at home

because he refused to go to school.
You helped him sneak Ned, the barn dog,
into his room the night of the storm,

and gave him his first velocipede
(the one he fled the four bears on).
In genealogies I sought your bird bones,

found only great-grandfather's second wife,
a widow he married in 1868.
I named my daughter after you, and she

her daughter. Often we talk of you.
Another great-grandmother quilted her dreams
in taffeta and velvet.

But I like to imagine you an eagle
flying to the moon.

My Grandmother's Cinderella Tale

A motherless child of four
on a wind-swept lea of Anglesey,
she plaited garlands for imaginary playmates
from roses rioting her cottage roof,
raced dreams down pathways ribbed with silver,
saw in bright pools
tiaras for her touseled head,

Her only friends the terns,
swallows of the sea, taught her to dig
for playthings torn by tides
from distant wrecks—a velvet gown,
a doll with sapphire eyes,
a string of amethysts.

At seventeen she laid two Bibles
side by side to learn another tongue,
crossed the "pond" alone.
A kitchen maid, she crept
from the Cabots' scullery
into my grandfather's merry heart.

When he lifted her high on Blue Hill,
he laughed at her seabird cries,
made her promise never to tame
her wild Welsh lilt.
And she didn't until he died.

The Dishes of My Grandmother's Two Lives

Pale patrician, blue-veined with stylized vines,
a hallmarked platter posed proud
on the plate rail; in its center, a scene
serene as marble tableau under glass:
    small boy, Ganymede in frock coat,
    proffers a goblet to guests
    stiff as effigies on a tomb.

On the sideboard stocked with linen and lace
sat a rival artifact:
gaudy Welsh saucer, its leek blossoms
fanned to white fire by blue blaze
of wind-tossed waves.

Ghost of my grandmother,
whatever made you flee the green gold of Anglesey,
where light-dazzled curlews roamed midnight skies,
to roost in a dark parlor far across the sea?

My Mother as a Young Girl

Mounted on her Boston rocker,
Great-aunt Eliza, armored in black bombazine,
tilted with young Margaret, seven
the year her beloved father died.

    Tall, wild-iris-eyed, he'd been the darling
    of Eliza's heart until he "stained their blood
    wedding that ignorant Welsh servant girl
    he'd romanced in the Cabots' kitchen."
    And Eliza could not forget.

    She vowed on the family Bible inscribed by
    Ebenezars, Ezekials, Zebediahs
    never to cross his threshold
    nor bless their tainted seed.

    But at his funeral, hearing
    the schoolmarm at Ponkapoag Primary
    dub Margaret "quick's a lightning bug
    at her *McGuffey Reader*," she'd relented,

    said she'd have the girl to tea, and if she
        measured up,
    see to her manners, even to a proper education,
    provided, of course, she did not
    utter her sluttish mother's name.

Little Margaret, ankles crossed,
toes straight ahead, took her tea
in tiny sips, flicked her lips
with point of napkin, began to talk about

the mother who told bed time tales
fanciful as the Jack Frost panes she stitched
in linens with thread so fine
you couldn't even see it, changed seaweed
to a pudding white as snow and barnyard eggs
to flan that always made her father
thump his thigh and sigh,
"Best little cook this side of heaven."

Great-aunt Eliza, knuckles clenched, shut her eyes,
rocked her steed until it creaked,
while Margaret chattered on.

My Mother's Alchemy

for Margaret Fisher Williams, 1885–1957

It's midmorning on what's supposed to be
the first day of spring. From a window in the house
where I was born, I'm peering for some sign of it—
flush of robin, crocus piercing snow.

Suddenly, memories of my mother's alchemy:

> These hunched old trees once sprouted
> iron rings, a rope to shinny
> hand over faltering hand;
>
> this lawn, a chinning bar, a balance beam,
> a tall toboggan slide for flying wind blind;
> for swaying self-esteem, a rungless ladder
> (two poles held by oaks that scooped the sky).

Memories of her voice:

> A drooping spine?
> A drooping life.
>
> The backbone in slumping Russ?
> Chin in, stretch tall,
> smile smile smile.
>
> The grace in clumsy Grace?
> Heel, toe, run run run
> skip to my loo, my darling.

The common sense in harebrained me?
Swing low, let the old cat die
before you loop the loop.

Shadowed on the spring snow
branches and twigs from the towering trunks—
all the lives she tended in her sun.

Tigress

Barn chores done, light fading fast,
I climb the forbidden ladder
to my secret nest within the bales.

What is that cry
like rasp of leaf on pane
that rises from the mow?

A tiny point of ear,
jagged as if bitten,
pokes above just-opened eyes.

From coil of orphan kittens,
stiff paws still curled for kneading,
I pull a living mite of tiger cat
whose newborn lips nurse air.

I nest it in one mittened hand,
put the other hand on shaky rung,
and shudder down a glowering of rats.

Outside the barn under blackening sky,
brute wind beats me back,
once-friendly willow wands claw
my face with witches' fingers.

A cry of kitten rises from my throat.
On stone legs as in a dream
I stumble without moving . . .

until a purr, tiger strong,
tugs us both
to nest in light.

In the Portrait of the Sisters

for Liz, beloved imp, 1913–1995

In the portrait of the sisters
on the living room wall
you wear a Mona Lisa smile
as you aim a pointed satin toe
at a rosebud fallen from
Charlotte's basket. With your
hand you push away the landscape
behind you: a poplar-bordered stream
reflecting ruins of a castle and
snow-capped mountaintop.

You were always leading us
down byways from the beaten path:
      "C'mon, Fraidy Cat,
      cross the street with me
      to see those banty roosters
      with their fuzzy leggings.
      No one will ever know."
But Mrs. Pinkerton did
when she saw the bloody claw mark
just above your lips
and painted it with iodine.
"Wrong brings wrong,"
you smiled, mimicking mother.

You played a wry Pied Piper
when, for cultural enrichment
we visited New York.
You took small Stella by the hand
and chanted back at prim and proper me

30

mincing like a matron up Fifth Avenue:
"Ve vant da candy and da gum.
Ve vant da candy and da gum."
You were the only one who dared
hang by your ankles
from the monkey bars
free as a cloud
from fear of falling.
Yet you chanced to break one wrist
and, one week later, the other
on the way to school— just before
the recital in the church,
where you smirked from a pew
as my fingers jarred
rebel sevenths from Mozart's *Minuet in G.*

And you giggled recklessly
when you and Eleanor Goetz
attacked the yellow jackets' nest,
threw hard-boiled eggs down the clothes chute,
used Gramma Fisher's folded, ironed
cleaning cloths to scrub your tricycles,
prettified the playhouse with bunches of
Miss Pickett's dahlias she told us
had been sown by angels.

Riches Gained on the Way

for Charlotte, sister who shares them still

Better that . . . when you reach the island you are old
rich with all you have gained on the way.

—C.P. Cavafy

i

Dinard

Belgian lace curtains
opening on the bay

field of fishing boats
blossoming in morning sun

daisies on clawfoot stand
beneath the window

On small night table
pen and notebook waiting

for tidal messages

ii

Paris

mimosa mingling
with leaf mold

iron hinge scraping
ancient courtyard door

loose shutter syncopating
muffled laughter

On wide white sill
pot of basil, bowl of plums

worn copy of
La Bohemè

Family Rocker

You were hewn by thinking hands
that knew the ways of wood:
how fresh-cut pine swells
with the seasons

until it bonds with hickory;
how sugar maple
shapes a spindle tough enough
to brace a tired spine;

how arms of wood feel
a cradler's hidden need
for cradling and for dreams
to spin a body to the moon.

Watching my mother's seasons fall
like drops from pole of gondolier,
I used to think she listened
for a serenade or tarantella,

but now I know
she listened for
the barcarole you rocked
for her mother's mother's mother.

In This Hallowed Cove

Where waters of Lake Butte des Morts
mingle with the Fox, our father told us
how Menominees, Gatherers of Wild Rice,
saw in the northern lights
spirits of shamans dancing praise
for golden panicles that send
nourishing seeds from tall reeds.

In this same cove at summer's end,
as wisps of my children's bonfire
join the solar flares, I shiver
at dark clumps of marsh uprooted
from their river home, and at the glint
of broken glass in oily pools.

I see in the holy lights
a danse macabre of ghosts
bewildered and forlorn, blown like rags
round and round black holes in space.

Emma's Christening Gown

This long gown yellowed by time,
found in a musty attic trunk,
bore a note carefully pinned:
"Grandma Fisher's christening dress."

Soaked overnight in Mrs. Beeton's brew
of nostrums and boiling water,
its hand spun lace emerged white
as the snows to come on Emma's christening day.

This minus zero Sunday, doubt gusts in
on January wind: Can cloth sheer as mousseline
hide a fleecy bunting, or human hands
squeeze its bulk through openings

elfin as these? But a bundled little Emma,
weightless as a sunbeam,
smiles trustingly as invisible
hands glide her through.

Grandma Sitting Emma

She sails along the way a dream does,
veering off course to touch
the heirloom demitasse set
on the peacock tray.

A tiny handle fits her thumb,
its golden rim, her lips that sip
like a bee from honeysuckle chalice.

I wag a firm no.
She wags in imitation,
reluctantly returns cup to saucer.

Then she spins the bow
of her small boat,
aiming it arrow straight
to the harbor of my arms.

On Little John's Baptismal Day

My father saw no need
for sanctuaried rituals,
his garden, church enough.
Baptismal font a birdbath
where orioles and wrens
splashed themselves with sky.

At twelve, in chancel hidden
by clematis, creeping thyme,
and scarlet runner beans,
all by myself—except for audience
of hummingbird and honeybee—
I bowed my head, and felt
the touch of dew that opens
morning glories to the sun.

Today I watch the baptism
of Baby John who's much too young
to understand the laying on of hands,
but not too young to feel the laving of the light.

Thank You Note to My Granddaughter

for Lisa

Like April you surprise
the tired old winter in me,
shoot up the mercury,
put new lenses in my eyes
that paint the grey world blue,
reveal those speckled eggs
the mourning dove has left
for a brief flutter in the sun.
Suddenly things I've never
understood spring into bloom.

That Fieldmouse Stare

Half asleep when moving into Monday,
I gathered from my motherpath
bear cub with button nose, Lincoln Log,
clutch of clay, teething ring,

and something warm and silken,
something I didn't recognize until
a twitch of hairless tail and a dry old
cellar smell made me want to hurl it
and go back to sleep.

Instead, the panic in its eyes
made me press it to my cheek
and murmur, "There, there."
All the while, Felix smiled his Cheshire grin.

Years later in a crowded hall at school
as I rushed to meet my class before the bell,
I saw that fieldmouse stare again in eyes
that could not hide from smirks that pummeled,
that left no catscratch signs, but brought a small,
unnoticed death to Monday morning.

Watching Old Fat Cat

Fat Cat, as I watch you
half-dozing on the velvet chair,
the pussy willow paws
that curled around so many kittens
tucked benignly under your chin,

the black pupils in your green eyes
thinner now than thorns of a rose,
I can't forget watching you
watching that tremor of grass
that crouched you noiseless.

You unsheathed your claws,
widened each pupil to an onyx moon,
eclipsing whatever sun existed
for the star-nosed mole.

Pup

with granddaughter Chris

Even in his name
he was unpretentious.
He made no claim
to be a dog-show swell,

shampooed and svelte
mincing around a track
with tail held high or low
depending on the fashion.

It was windy and cold
when we found him
hiding beside the lane
between the Yakima apple trees

where a sage bush huddled
out of place in rows
where only apples dared to grow.

He parted his lips
in a knowing smile
as if sure we were destined
to find him.

Someone had to take him in
we said, and did
for we were not yet five.

We never figured how old he was
when his coat began to gray,
when he seldom tried to jump
because he'd trip,

but the look in his eyes stayed as
bright as it was when he found us
and took us in.

The Hornets Speak

This old gym is our empire.
Its height only we can soar.
Darting between blades

of whirring fans, rising
with the speed of light
to our queen's secret throne,

we watch with narrowing eyes
the clumsy floor-bound creatures
who, with stomp of heavy sole,

splay to smeared spots
our gossamer wings.
Our shining striped bodies,

intricately joined
by our wasp waists,
they drop, grinning,

bowing to applause,
into the muck of trash cans,
already the graves

of graying styrofoam cups
and other corpses
they've discarded.

Rejected Foal

I knew I had to save him
when I saw him standing all alone
watching his mother's milk
gush out in a pale blue stream.

Holding his sprout of mane,
I teased his lips with rubber dug,
even tried to imitate a nicker.
But his soft mouth hardened.

Nostrils flaring, he thrashed side to side,
stomped smoke, glared fire,
sent the bottle flying,
a sticky lure for flies.

When he wrenched off
to gnaw on splinters,
my nerves crumbling, I sank down
on a nearby bale of straw.

Motionless as brooding hen,
I must have hunched there all afternoon
in cloud of gnat, steam of hay
until he sidled near in shy slow steps

to lay his heavy neck upon my own
in the way of mares on sunny days,
or of drays fused against
the snow and sleet of winter.

II

LIGHT IN THE DARKNESS

On First Reading Neruda

The poems I used to ride, their sleek manes
combed and shining, loped familiar lanes
where shadows played with light.

But the day you threw me,
the world beneath the world trembled,
heaved huge boulders through the holes in space.

Sky raged below, massive roots
reached to strangle chimneys,
your mane sprang up and crackled.

Leaves writhed in the firestorm of your stomping.
An acorn and the singed wing of a moth
fused with your hoofprint on my skull.

Missed Deadline

Late, late. Already
the ninth chime of the twelve.
Frantic, I race time for
my golden coach and eight,
slip on the crystal stair,
lose to midnight my slipper of silver
and spun-glass self.

The hungry moon sucking my light
is a grinning pumpkin.
With the heavy sole
of my wooden shoe
I smash it,
throw its seeds
to the red-eyed mice,

flee
to the cold smolder
of cinders.

Netting the Words

Day's glare softens to violet.
Once-loved twilit words
—*hirondelle lavande* crepuscule—

sweep down like swallows
readying for flight
on waiting wires.

Night-blooming nicotiana
and moonflowers release hints
of subterranean springs.

Suddenly on the trembling leaf
of my writing hand
a chrysalis.

The Unicorn Today

Long ago when the unicorn's hooves
thundered from the forest's heart, heads bowed.

That was before merchants noosed him
to lead parades of jaded innocence,

and better shops proclaimed him in;
before mannequins, wimpled and demure,

groveled at his vine-wreathed hocks,
caressed his sequined neck;

before his alabaster horn became
a lance for tidbits *en brochette,*

and his otherworldly eyes
began to peer from plastic plates.

When his clones leered from toilet tissue,
he fled beyond the mists of myth

which part only when his thunder
echoes from a poet's song.

Half-remembered Dreams of Ancient Nights

Earth, gone wanton,
has shed her robe of white—
unfolds, yawns, aches
under the gaze of April moon.

Hyacinths perfume her languid breath,
ferns caress her arcing breasts.
Half-remembered dreams of ancient nights
stir her waking.

October

Sharp blades of sumac,
roadside scarlet as a cry—
August's aftermath.

Blue spruce mourners sigh
on the banks of *Roche à Cri*—
summer's elegy.

On the road ahead,
calligraphy of winter—
three ebony crows.

One lone juniper
climbing wall of solid stone—
does it have no roots?

On tall tamarack—
black hawk studying meadows,
choosing his sparrow.

Scrub oak carnival—
each crooked twig and wild leaf
inventing its dance.

Defiers of wind—
saplings of birch and poplar
prance on precipice.

Mississippi bluff
pointing north west south east—
compass of my dreams.

Now in the Fox River Valley

Barns do not sleep
as they used to
under quilts of darkened sky

when evening caressed them,
tucked shadows round their ridges,
lulled them with sparrow vespers.

Mother Night, Argus-eyed,
stares their dreams to nightmares
with her vapor lights.

Progress

When the old Jones farm
succumbed to urban sprawl, no battle—
only the scritch of Owen's pen
as he signed away his kingdom:

his citadel, the barn,
lightning rods reared fierce,
had towered all his years
over Holstein strongholds,

bright alfalfa halls
and corridors of corn,
passageways for
partridges and quail.

Silent his cohorts:
vacant stanchions,
empty hayracks
swaying in the wind,
sunflowers with
bowed heads.

The Day the Silo Fell

Months before it fell,
no longer rich with fodder,
the empty silo listed west,
seeping dust of mortar.

No child dared hide
where only echoes lived.
One night a steer that wandered in
to graze silvered lichen

swelled larger than the door and died entombed.
The day it fell, milkhouse windows
cracked, the barn shuddered,
pigeons froze on tall beams.

I swear I saw the sky split
and heard the beat
of pterodactyl wings.

Miss Violet's Spruces

Eighty years now Miss Violet's shaped
her spruces like little igloos
to give them a Mother Goose look,

cut back their bright green quills
each spring since she started to teach
first grade at Lone Elm Primary.

Each night she's dreamed
      Bobby Shafto's gone to sea—
      He'll come back and marry me.

As bent and shriveled as she,
Bo Peep and Margery Daw
shake thin grey locks

at the hulking monsters
with their sharp-toothed snouts
that bulldoze all her trees away.

Evening

White shadows hover,
bend to pat her shawl,
arrange thinning tassels
on her husk of cheek.

She no longer heeds the chiding
of the clock and barely makes out
what the nanny nurses say:
>"She's reading upside down again."
>"She's smiling at TV."

They don't know she smiles at
what lies behind her eyes:
country beyond dream
where half a century he cradled

her in his strong arms,
and where his searching lips
will mute her own
before they swallow sky.

Lament

after an old photograph found in the attic

When elderberries ripened
in the yellow sun
Thunderbirds from above the clouds
swept him away

Two moons she fasted
laced her braids blue
spoke only to his buckskins
bundled at her breast

The elders commanded
    Cease mourning
    Choose another
    to fill you with seed

To Mother Sun she sprinkled prayermeal
bowed before Midnight Moon
begged the Great Birds
    Take me to him

They only swooped
to beat purple wings
on the darkening
rim of sky

Her heart
a small bird
has followed them
through the roof of the world

She stands
a sandstone widow
waiting for his voice
in the wind

Full Face

1840–1925

Between red velvet album covers
filigreed in gold
peer faces,

some demure as violets,
some tiger lily proud.
Most turn aslant

from draped tripods
hiding photographers.
But here, full face,

is Sarah Lawson Ramsay,
patience incarnate in a gaze
proclaiming how

things that change stay the same
for all who've tasted heaven
in a cooing sound.

Of her sixteen children, eight would die
before they entered school.
But she would live

to feel their rhythms rising
as a dozen mothers
sang her lullabies.

Holding Still

Old Willoughby, bent double on the wicker chair
that's been on the back porch
since he was a boy,

still casts for memories:
the gangling Holstein calf
clutched squirming on the back seat

of his father's Ford at midnight,
to sneak it beneath the Hereford
before she sensed her own was dead;

Number Nine, the two-ton Shorthorn bull
that ambled every evening to the fence
for the stroking of his massive brow;

the three-legged tiger cat
pulled from the stock tank
just before her thirteenth litter;

Tess, first of the pointers, cradling
first pheasant in her trembling jaws
as if it were a pup;

and Prince, stallion of the silver mane,
skimming the bog behind the barn,
then holding still

for the picking of wild
just-ripening plums.

Clear Winding Deeps

for Felicia Krance, 1909–1993

At times when burdocks
block my hopes
and nettles sting my dreams,

I think of Fela at eighty-five
suited for her daily swim
striding down weedy path

to sandy banks above
clear winding deeps
I never knew were there.

The Same Sun

for Anne Coyle Howard, 1915–1994

i

The sun that slithered impishly
through purple plumes of broom
lured you toward a gate barbed with iron

and froze me, eyes fixed on your braids
shining red-gold as they flounced ahead
straight toward the old troll watchman

shaking blackness from huge keys
clenched tight; that oaken door in Devon
hiding behind its sign, Travelers Beware.

That same sun sends me, steady now, to follow
your braids, white as a dream of whiteness,
beyond the dooms of dark.

ii

Now that skies have closed around you,
I see your glow reflected in memories:

> Once we biked tandem
> the wild upper path
> around Loch Katrine
>
> and the black shore
> of the bottomless tarn
> known to suck fools in.

With you I shunned
traveled passageways
when seeking destinations

that alone,
too timorous to dream of,
I would not seek, nor can . . .

until your spirit
draws mine up
to alpine meadows.

Something Unfenced

for Gudrun Garmacher, 1904–1994

i

Eyes closed, fingers motionless
as the icicles your windows weep.
All week you've lain, pale flower
on sheets white as the snow on kneeling
trees in the Pleasant Acres courtyard.

Gladys sits in your favorite chair
brought from Fourth Street Road
where your trolls beamed in firelights
as, year on year, her daily voice
refreshed your roots with tales.

This winter evening your daughter/mother
turns the pages as she used to while your needles
flew on Rockford afternoons.

When she pauses to stroke your brow,
the petals of your face glow,
an amaryllis opening.

ii

Sometimes these twilight years
I pull down shades, close my eyes,
huddle in the dark.

The memory of your inward smile
makes me open curtains

67

to soft air and small boys

skipping smooth stones
from willow banks to meadows
framed in fences long forgotten.

I see something unfenced
wandering a green hill
like thistledown, into a silence
of just-blooming stars.

Hush Before Winter

i

Slowly , slowly, the twelve bur oaks in this yard
release their families of leaves—
    some scalloped like old Clarissa's doilies,
    some sharp edged as Aunt Eliza's tongue.

Already they have loosed on lawn and driveway
myriad acorns—
    some in monk-caps, tonsures hidden,
    some in bonnets, wisping curls.

The melding of their progeny
with furrowed bark, roots and stems
they trust to mothering darkness.

ii

A breeze stirs the slow descent
of enormous maple leaves
drifting to the pavement
this October afternoon.

A dry oak straggler
brittle as a beetle
somersaults around them
—Nijinski leaping toward the sun—

pauses only long enough
to gather from its veined heart
the gusto for a *tour jeté*

iii

You cannot tell the ages of these trees
unless you cleave them
to count their rings,

their limbs nets
to catch
millennia of sky.

The First of the Twelve Great Oaks to Fall

She sank slowly,
grazing the front porch roof and steps,
blocking the driveway.

In the crook
of two branches
a nest of jays—

eyes unopened,
small beaks gaping wide
for mashed seed.

No cankers or warts
on her breathing bark.
No tunneling roots

like those of her sister trees.
Hers reached up
as if to feed on air.

Wise Up, Old Fool

You've been looking for hours, days even,
for that bathrobe belt, the one that
holds you decent mornings,
for the crab soufflé recipe
in last week's paper,

the file on how to program the VCR
and work the wireless stereo headphones,
the note you wrote in the night
on how one dream echoes another,
the clipping on why an oak
still fresh and green
falls on a windless day
while an ash outlives a hurricane.

Months ahead, when you least expect,
what's lost will emerge from fold of towel
or pile of bills postponed.

Wise up, Old Fool,
stop climbing cobweb ladders.
While you still have sight,
watch earth emerge from shawl of snow,
coax out trillium.

If you watch long enough,
you're bound to find
the diamond from your wedding ring
shining in the rain.

Daughter

I am watching you,
still life framed by white window
in this darkening light.

Behind you,
fan-shaped branches of an ailanthus
sway slowly.

Air alone choreographs
the tremulous spreading and lifting
of tapered leaves.

No need to speak.
Like the still air,
you stir my heart to dancing.

Life Epic

Carnation garland
plaited for my wedding veil,
its spice lingers still.

On cold attic floor
wheels of a pink tricycle
motionless.

Coat open, on lap
button box overflowing.
Not one matches.

You who spilled grape juice
on my white damask chair
now steady my cup.

To Whom It May Concern

The young don't know
how thread misses
even the needle threader's eye,
the needle itself floating away
into a surf of carpet;

how shopping lists drift off
east of the sun west of the moon
along with names of cousins,
titles of favorite books,
dates of birthdays;

how nonsense rhymes unbidden,
each syllable exact, croak off-key
from a cracking throat . . .

> *Old Dan Tucker was a funny old man,*
> *he washed his face in a frying pan,*
> *he combed his hair with a wagon wheel*
> *and died with a toothache in his heel.*

Yet, just as unexpectedly,
shining memories burst
from the undertow of time,
dolphins leaping.

As I Turn Eighty

for John

These days what's on the tip of my tongue
escapes, especially dates of cosmic happenings
like the deaths of oak and elms.

You, eighty-four, still know the way
to Slough Bridge in the dead of night,
to the willow lane where moonlight

reveals a family of deer grazing
at the far edge of the wheat field
where you used to canter King.

You tell me to take my time,
not give up the search
for all those names that will return,

shyly stepping like fawns at dawn
if they're not shouted for:
the name of that first shorthorn filly

born in the barn at midnight;
of the calf that would have won a "blue"
if he hadn't been so small;

of the "safe" plodding mare
retired from camp Hiawela
that spooked my brains

into the rock pile that windy noon,
scattering my modicum of common sense
to the racing clouds.

The Grandmothers in Aerobics Class

They slump against gym wall tugging
reluctant sneakers over millstone feet.
The aerobics hour is about to begin.

Outside a shrill Wisconsin wind shrieks warning.
They do not belong in this country of the young
where heart rates soar.

Gravity, torpor, and common sense hold them bound
until the boombox beat of Lionel Richie's
"Dancing on the Ceiling" bounces them free.

Botticellian light washes the frost off windows,
and orange trees entwined with laurel
rise from the varnished floor.

The grandmothers feel themselves transforming.
Dowager humps and mottles fading, they become
the sylph-like Graces of the Primavera.

On weightless feet they skim soft petals
flung by their leader, the demi-goddess
with the demon grin, who whirls them through
the rites of spring—she their mirror,
her leaps and dips their own.

When cooldown music ends the enchanted hour
with "Memory," that mournful tune from *Cats*,
they suddenly remember what the wind has cried,
and a momentary shiver shakes their thinning bones.

But, wrapped in reawakened rhythms,
their bodies singing still,
the springstruck grandmothers glide out
to dance down winter.